books by
BOX____

www.booksbyboxer.com

Published by
Books By Boxer, Leeds, LS13 4BS UK
Books by Boxer (EU), Dublin D02 P593 IRELAND
© Books By Boxer 2022
All Rights Reserved
MADE IN CHINA
ISBN: 9781909732629

**Paint your toilet brown with this unique swatch book –
and say hello to your fragrant new room!**

With 50 uniquely c**p shades of brown and their inspiration,
you can dribble, splash, and splatter some colour all around
your bathroom.

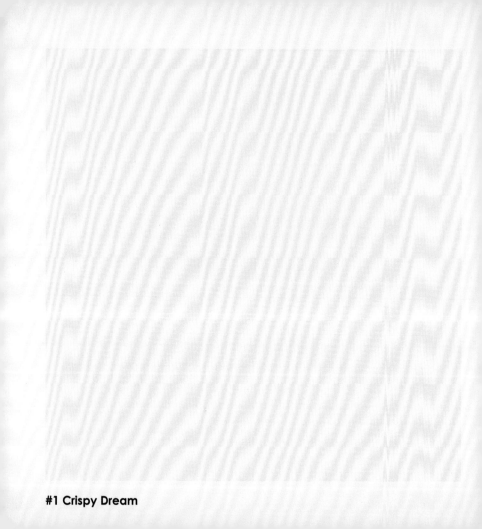

#1 Crispy Dream

Proof that a solid and versatile shade doesn't have to cost a *packet*. However, every rose has its thorn, and this shade, albeit smooth and easy to apply, is still a little rough around the edges.

#2 Sanding Block

Bring the beach to your bathroom with this fast-drying and versatile shade. Its thick and gritty consistency is perfect for adding a subtle, sandy texture to your bathroom.

#3 Caramel Latte

A sweet and creamy shade that will complement most bathroom furniture. Why not give it an extra pump for an even more intense caramel aesthetic?

#4 Burlap Sack

An earthy and versatile shade that is not for the novice decorator, as it is often mistakenly applied to the wrong bathroom utensils. In case of an incorrect application, do not allow to dry, wipe any affected surfaces immediately.

#5 Mystery Mocha

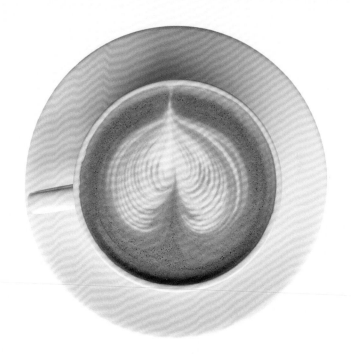

Make a *Grande* entrance with this coffee and chocolate fusion inspired shade that will certainly take you and your bathroom vistors by surprise.

#6 Vintage Cork

Add a fizzy and fun pop of colour to your bathroom with this excitingly refreshing hue. When you finally start applying this shade, you'll find it hard to stop.

Did you hear about the constipated mathematician?

He worked it out with a pencil.

In World War 2, German tank drivers in Africa used to drive tanks over camel poo for good luck. When Allies got wind of this, they then planted land mines disguised as camel poo, to take down the German tanks!

#7 Treacle Pudding

Light and airy, and renowned for its stickiness, this classic shade will suit most modern bathrooms, and is often complemented with a cream or custard.

#8 Turtlehead Bay

A confidently risky shade that will show others that you have finally come out of your shell. Ideal for permanent applications, as this shade is irreversible.

#9 Forest Fungus

Perfect for smaller bathrooms, this shade will open up the space when there isn't *mushroom* available. Suitable for use in damp areas with little to no light.

#10 Seeded Bagel

A shade that is perfect for introducing a little texture to your bathroom. Just remember to clean your utensils thoroughly after use, otherwise you'll have a *hole* load of trouble.

#11 Runny Honey

Causing you to make a *bee*-line for the bathroom, this sticky-sweet surprise will transform your toilet into a hive of activity.

#12 Fresh Croissant

Bathroom décor getting you down? Thinking of redecorating? Well there's no time like the *crescent*. This freshly baked shade will only need a single application to make you feel *all butter*.

#13 Korma Chameleon

Known to incite the urge to *come and go,* this intriguing shade appears to change every time you look.

#14 Chocolate Rain

Bring a little Jackson Pollock to your bathroom with this sweet shade that's straight from another *Galaxy*. Its watery composition makes it ideal for creating uniquely artistic splatter patterns. Best applied with a spray bottle.

#15 Turkish Delight

A *Sha*-warmer shade that will be sure to bring a little Middle Eastern heat to your bathroom.

#16 Hanging Hazelnut

Dropping soon is this thrillingly tense shade that will certainly add some colourful anticipation to your bathroom, and keep you hanging on by a thread.

#17 Marbled Ember

A shade that is sometimes described as being 2 colours in 1, this devilishly deceptive duo will leave you guessing as to which shade left you feeling all warm and fuzzy inside.

Poop jokes aren't my favourite jokes.

But they're a solid #2.

The most expensive toilet ever made is quite literally out of this world! It is fitted in the International Space Station, and cost around 19 million dollars!

#18 Bad Penny

A budget option, but still a perfect example to prove that a good shade doesn't have to cost the earth, as long as you can ignore the pungent, metallic aroma.

#19 Cloth Touch

A thrilling and versatile hue that is born purely out of desperation, this shade is best applied as a series of thin coats to achieve the desired effect. Keep away from fabric surfaces as this shade may stain.

#20 Copper Rocket

Take your bathroom to infinity and beyond with this *ass-tronomic* shade that will be sure to help you blast-off in style (and avoid any black holes).

#21 Mexican Standoff

Drawing inspiration from the fiery traditional cuisine of South America, your bathroom will be the *taco* the town when this spicy shade is *jalapeño* toilet.

#22 Olive Branch

Sitting comfortably on the border between brown and green, this shade is often overlooked and regularly underestimated to great lengths.

#23 Acorn Ambience

A natural and earthy shade inspired by the nuts and seeds
typically found stored in the cheeks of a squirrel,
not a person...

#24 Spicy Surprise

Spontaneously and without much warning, bring the heat to your bathroom with a shade that is sure to take you, and other bathroom visitors, by surprise.

#25 Beaver Dam

A popular choice for the ladies, this shade will liven up any dull bathroom. Given its erratic consistency, extra care must be taken when cleaning up after applying, remembering to always clean brushes front to back, not back to front.

#26 Conker String

Bring some autumnal nostalgia to your bathroom with this shade that will certainly cause you to reminisce about swinging your string, without smashing your seeds.

#27 Toffee Star

A subtle golden shade that may once have seemed out of reach. However, with a bit of perseverance and a lot of luck, you may finally be able to apply this decadent tone to your bathroom after all.

#28 Bucket Rust Umber

A bright and vibrant shade that clings to surfaces like rust on a bucket, perfect for adding a little vintage patina to your bathroom furniture.

One friend, confiding in another, said, "I take a poop every morning at 8 a.m."

"Hey, it's good to be regular. What's the problem?" Replied the other.

"I wake up at 9 a.m." Admitted the first.

The average person spends a total of three years of their life on the toilet, which explains why approximately 7 million mobile phones are dropped down the toilet every year!

#29 Weathered Saddle

Is your bathroom furniture looking tired and over-worked?
If so, this shade is perfect for a simple budget refresh, just
remember: to avoid splinters or trapped appendages,
smooth all surfaces before applying.

#30 Corn Speckle

A much-loved classic, this charming and characterful shade pairs perfectly with yellow accents, and will make your bathroom look and feel *a-maize-ing*.

#31 Fiery Cinnabar

A solid, warm, and glossy shade with complementary hues of the deepest red. Apply sparingly and with great care, there is no need to *pile* this shade on as it is already positively *bursting* with vibrancy.

#32 Carob Phantom

A notoriously elusive and understated shade that finds itself better suited floating around in the dark, subterranean labyrinths of your bathroom.

#33 Doughnut Sprinkle

When it comes to adding a sprinkle of sweet decadence to your bathroom, this shade is the *holey* grail. Apply generously and *doughnut* forget to wipe away any excess.

#34 Baked Cupcake

Increasing in popularity due to the ever changing busy modern lifestyle, this decadently rich shade is so satisfying, you'll want to use it all in one go, but why not seal it up and save some for later?

#35 Electric Eel

Electrify your *excremities* with this shockingly slippery shade that will make any guests *f-eel* a little *jelly* of your bathroom décor. In fact, your toilet will become so popular, you'll have to start *charging* for entry.

#36 Roasted Loaf

A warm and earthy shade that will incite memories of your mother's cooking every time you step inside your bathroom. Patch test recommended as the colour may differ when dry.

#37 Tough Mudder

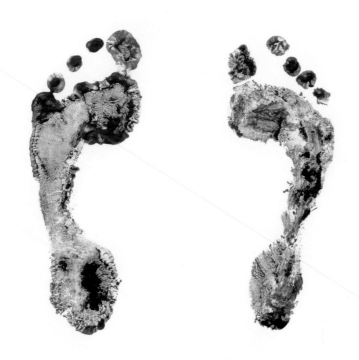

Known in the industry for its excellent coverage coupled with its difficult application, this shade is definitely best suited to professionals only.

#38 Beer Bottle

Sharpen up the aesthetic of your bathroom with this painfully stylish shade. For a neater finish, mask your ceiling to avoid any mess whilst cutting in.

#39 Brown Mamba

Add a *slither* of jungle style to your bathroom with this serpent inspired shade. Best applied from a distance to avoid clogging up your decorating utensils.

Why did the baker have smelly hands?

He kneaded a poo.

Some people get 'book bowels', a condition called 'Mariko Aoki phenomenon' which makes you have the urge to poo after smelling books...

(better get sniffing this book!)

#40 Figgy Pudding

Fancy introducing a festive feel to your bathroom? This shade has the perfect balance of warmth and winter, and has the ideal consistency and coverage to match. Just keep away from open flames, as it may be set alight!

#41 Golden Ticket

Guaranteed to turn your bathroom into *a world of pure imagination*. But don't hold your breath, you'll be lucky to secure this shade as only 5 batches have ever been produced by the factory.

#42 Cocoa Canoe

Incorporate a more nautically inspired theme into your bathroom with this positively buoyant and uplifting shade that will help you unwind as you watch all your worries float away... then reappear moments later.

#43 Mole Hole

This bittersweet shade takes great inspiration from the deep, dark, bottomless tones of *mole-asses*. Much the same in consistency as it is in colour, the dense and treacly compostion makes this best suited for use with advanced decorating equipment only.

#44 Mahogany Beads

A deep and rich shade that is only available in small amounts due to its dense concentration. However, don't let its size fool you, a little can go a long way to improve the look and feel of your bathroom.

#45 Lucky Limpet

A timeless classic that certainly stuck around when other shades were washed away. This shade is fast-drying and water resistant, so may need a little extra brush of encouragement when cleaning.

#46 Bakelite Telephone

With vintage tones not dissimilar to the plastic telephones of days gone by, this warm and nutty shade is sure to keep you hanging on the line for some time.

#47 Bronze Age

The perfect balance of old and new, this shade is ideal for bathrooms that haven't been redecorated for a disproportionate length of time.

#48 Loose Liquorice

A shade with *allsorts* of suitable applications, the most commonly favoured being the bathroom. Where certain other shades may be tough, this one is the perfect consistency to ensure a smooth application.

#49 Walnut Stool

If your bathroom is a place of quiet contemplation, then this shade is perfect for helping you to relax and unwind whilst you're having a *sit* on the toilet.

#50 Bitter Stout

Perfectly matched to the national beverage of the Emerald Isle, this shade will certainly leave visitors to your bathroom gasping for *Éire*.

Yesterday I ate four tins of alphabet soup.

What followed was probably the biggest vowel movement
I've ever had.

There are 200 times less germs on a toilet seat than there are on a computer keyboard!

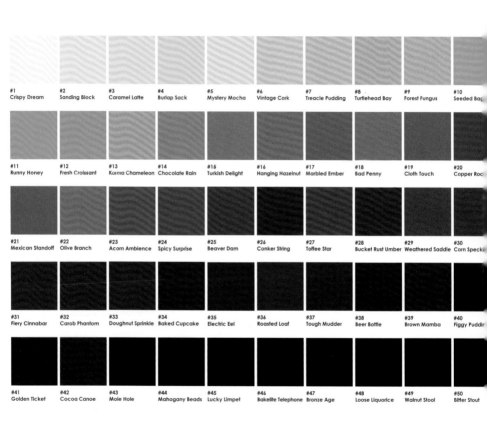

#1 Crispy Dream
#2 Sanding Block
#3 Caramel Latte
#4 Burlap Sack
#5 Mystery Mocha
#6 Vintage Cork
#7 Treacle Pudding
#8 Turtlehead Bay
#9 Forest Fungus
#10 Seeded Bap

#11 Runny Honey
#12 Fresh Croissant
#13 Korma Chameleon
#14 Chocolate Rain
#15 Turkish Delight
#16 Hanging Hazelnut
#17 Marbled Ember
#18 Bad Penny
#19 Cloth Touch
#20 Copper Rock

#21 Mexican Standoff
#22 Olive Branch
#23 Acorn Ambience
#24 Spicy Surprise
#25 Beaver Dam
#26 Conker String
#27 Toffee Star
#28 Bucket Rust Umber
#29 Weathered Saddle
#30 Corn Speckie

#31 Fiery Cinnabar
#32 Carob Phantom
#33 Doughnut Sprinkle
#34 Baked Cupcake
#35 Electric Eel
#36 Roasted Loaf
#37 Tough Mudder
#38 Beer Bottle
#39 Brown Mamba
#40 Figgy Puddin

#41 Golden Ticket
#42 Cocoa Canoe
#43 Mole Hole
#44 Mahogany Beads
#45 Lucky Limpet
#46 Bakelite Telephone
#47 Bronze Age
#48 Loose Liquorice
#49 Walnut Stool
#50 Bitter Stout